Birds

IMAGES OF HAWAI'I'S FEATHERED HERITAGE

Photography by H. Douglas Pratt, Tom Dove, and Jacob Faust

Mutual Publishing

Front cover: 'I'iwi by Tom Dove
Back cover: Red-tailed Tropicbird by Jacob Faust

ISBN-10: 1-56647-795-6
ISBN-13: 978-1-56647-795-6
Library of Congress Catalog Card Number: 2006927636

First Printing, April 2007
1 2 3 4 5 6 7 8 9

Mutual Publishing, LLC
1215 Center Street, Suite 210
Honolulu, Hawai'i 96816
Ph: 808-732-1709 / Fax: 808-734-4094
Email: info@mutualpublishing.com
www.mutualpublishing.com

Printed in China

The Nēnē, or Hawaiian Goose, is the State Bird of Hawai'i;
it shares ancestry with the familiar Canada Goose. DOUGLAS PRATT

The crimson 'Apapane can be seen easily in forests of Hawai'i Volcanoes National Park and other upland areas throughout the islands. TOM DOVE

The Red-footed Booby is one of Hawai'i's most familiar seabirds. The three booby species found in the islands were all known to the Hawaiians by the one-letter name, 'A. TOM DOVE

The Kōlea, or Pacific Golden Plover, nests in Alaska but spends
most of its year in Hawai‘i and other warm climates. Douglas Pratt

The Hawaiian Coot, or 'Alae Ke'oke'o, can be seen
on almost any pond in the islands. Douglas Pratt

The critically endangered Short-tailed Albatross can sometimes be seen at Midway Atoll. JACOB FAUST

This nesting Red-tailed Tropicbird shows off its beautiful satin-like plumage. Douglas Pratt

A yellow ʻAnianiau, found only on Kauaʻi, feeds in flowers of the native ʻōhiʻa lehua tree. Tom Dove

Confiding juvenile Kaua'i 'Elepaio often approach hikers along mountain trails. Douglas Pratt

A Black-footed Albatross relaxes in a bed of exotic sweet alyssum on Midway Atoll. DOUGLAS PRATT

A striking drake Northern Shoveler, one of the two most
common species of wintering ducks in Hawai'i. Tom Dove

The dapper Masked Booby is the rarest of Hawai'i's three booby species. DOUGLAS PRATT

The Hawaiian Stilt, or Ae'o, is endangered by conversion of freshwater wetlands to other uses. JACOB FAUST

The elegant ʻĀkohekohe, formerly called Crested Honeycreeper,
is now found only in remote rainforests of Maui. Tom Dove

The Hawai'i 'Amakihi has had to adapt to the arrival of foreign trees, such as this pine in Maui's Hosmer Grove. Douglas Pratt

The mallard-like Koloa, or Hawaiian Duck, is the only
year-round resident duck in the main Hawaiian Islands. Douglas Pratt

The Kaua'i 'Amakihi, a native honeycreeper, feeds on both nectar and insects. Tom Dove

The Palila, found only in māmane forests on Mauna Kea, is a Hawaiian honeycreeper that retains the finch bill of the group's ancestor. TOM DOVE

The pale form of the Hawaiʻi ʻElepaio, a native flycatcher,
is found in the same forests as the Palila on the Big Island. Tom Dove

Lovely and endearing Common Fairy-Terns (White Tern) can be seen in parks in Honolulu, where they lay their single egg on a bare branch, and feed the chick fish caught at sea. Douglas Pratt

Formerly called Hill Robin in Hawai'i, the Red-billed Leiothrix, introduced from Asia, brightens Hawai'i's forests with color and song. TOM DOVE

The Great Frigatebird, 'Iwa, inflates its throat balloon only during courtship, but can be seen anywhere in Hawai'i year round. DOUGLAS PRATT

This 'I'iwi shows how Hawai'i's native nectar-feeders pollinate flowers, such as this Kaua'i koli'i. Tom Dove

The Pueo (Short-eared Owl) can be seen by day as well as after dark. It is Hawai'i's only native owl. TOM DOVE

The rare Bristle-thighed Curlew (Kioea) winters in Hawai'i,
and can be seen at certain sites on O'ahu and on Moloka'i. JACOB FAUST

The drab-colored 'Ōma'o, a native thrush, enlivens forests
on the Big Island with its energetic singing. Tom Dove

The White-rumped Shama, a thrush introduced from southeast Asia,
is one of the finest singers in Hawai'i. JACOB FAUST

Black-crowned Night-Herons, or 'Auku'u, can sometimes be seen around
koi ponds at Hawaiian resorts. They are the islands' only native herons. Douglas Pratt

The striking Red-crested Cardinal is a familiar sight in Hawaiian resorts, where it is often called Brazilian Cardinal to indicate its origins in South America. DOUGLAS PRATT

This male and female Red Avadavat, formerly called Strawberry Finch, exemplify
the many small colorful finches introduced to the Hawaiian Islands. Tom Dove

The 'Akia Pōlā'au, with one of the most bizarre bills of any bird, is a honeycreeper that fills the niche of a sapsucker on the Big Island. TOM DOVE

The graceful White-tailed Tropicbird is a seabird that often circles over lush lowland valleys and high volcanic craters in Hawai'i. DOUGLAS PRATT

A close-up of a Red-footed Booby reveals the
delicate pastel colors of its facial skin. Douglas Pratt

The 'Io, or Hawaiian Hawk, is found only on the Big Island, where it hunts large insects and birds. TOM DOVE

A Black Noddy, Noio Kōhā, nests in a tree heliotrope. Douglas Pratt

A Japanese White-eye joins native honeycreepers in ʻōhiʻa lehua trees. Tom Dove

Introduced on the Big Island, the Kalij Pheasant from the Indian subcontinent exemplifies the many game birds brought to the islands for the benefit of hunters. DOUGLAS PRATT

The evocatively named Wandering Tattler was called 'Ūlili
by the Hawaiians in imitation of its plaintive call. Douglas Pratt

40

The striking Northern Pintail, known to the Hawaiians as Koloa Māpu,
is the most common migratory duck in the islands. TOM DOVE

The warbler-like Maui ʻAlauahio can be seen at Hosmer Grove in Haleakalā National Park. Tom Dove

This immature 'Ākepa, which will eventually be entirely bright orange, shows the slightly crossed bill tips it uses to extract insect larvae from 'ōhi'a leaf buds. Tom Dove

A Hawaiʻi ʻElepaio of the windward rainforest subspecies. DOUGLAS PRATT

Look for the Hawaiian subspecies of Common Moorhen,
'Alae 'Ula, in wetlands of Kaua'i and O'ahu. TOM DOVE

Laysan Albatrosses nest in the thousands on the Northwestern Hawaiian Islands, and in smaller numbers on Kaua'i and O'ahu. Douglas Pratt

A Red-tailed Tropicbird prepares to land on a seaside cliff. Tom Dove

One of the last photos ever taken of the ʻŌʻo ʻāʻā, the Kauaʻi ʻŌʻō, not seen since the 1980s and presumed extinct. Sadly, Hawaiʻi's avifauna has lost more species than any other. DOUGLAS PRATT